**PROFESSIONAL
RESOURCES**

W9-AXF-251

Supports
The Four-Blocks™
Literacy Model

Teaching
Guided Reading Strategies
with Transparencies

by **Gregg O. Byers**

Editors	Artist	Cover Design
Carol Layton	Wayne Miller	Julie Webb
Tracy Soles		

Carson-Dellosa Publishing Company, Inc.

Table of Contents

Story Frame

Help students organize what they know about the Guided Reading selection. Story Frames are a way for students to learn to summarize the important details of a book as they sort through what they have read and condense the information into a few sentences. Story Frames also provide an opportunity for students to see what types of events and details are needed in a story. The goal is for students to be able to transfer this knowledge to their own writing. (See an example of a completed Story Frame transparency on the next page.)

Uses

- Teach a "mini-lesson" on how important details such as characters, setting, etc., are to a story before the reading or rereading of the day's book. As a follow-up to discussing details, have students use the Story Frame reproducible to discuss and record information within cooperative groups. Then, as a whole group, have students from the cooperative groups volunteer information while you write it on the transparency.

- Use the reproducible to evaluate students' understanding of the selection of the week. Have students complete the Story Frame reproducible individually or as a whole class to test comprehension of the book.

- Cut apart the different sections of the reproducible (setting, character, problem, problem solved, ending) and give one section to each student in the room. Have each student find the answer to the part of the Story Frame that he received. As a whole group, ask all those with a particular part (such as *character*) to share what they wrote. Students can discuss if they agree or disagree with the answers and why. Or, have students write the answers and paste the sections to the bottom of an 8½" x 11" sheet of paper. Each student can draw a picture of that part of the story in the space at the top of the page. Compile the Story Frames to create a class book.

- As a follow-up to a book, divide students into pairs and have them change one element in the story, such as a character or the problem, and then write what they think might have happened because of the changes made to the story.

- After studying a unit of books, list the different book titles on sentence strips. Then, give one of the title strips and a reproducible to each cooperative group. Have the group secretly record the story elements on the reproducible (without naming the character/s.) Then, pin up the book titles and have students trade reproducibles among groups. Each group must decide which Story Frame goes with each title.

Lesson

Share the book, *Six-Dinner Sid**, with students, then divide them into cooperative groups. Have each group designate one member as the recorder and use the reproducible to record the elements in the story. After giving the groups a specific time period to complete the assignment, have all students come together to share their interpretations of the story elements.

*Six-Dinner Sid by Inga Moore: Aladdin Paperbacks, 1993. (Picture book, ages 4-8, 32 pp.) Sid is a clever, black cat with literally six lives. His six different owners discover his ploys when he catches a cold, and they each take him to the vet.

Story Frame

Title: Six-Dinner Sid

Author: Inga Moore

This story takes place on Aristotle Street.

Sid the cat **is an important character in the story who** has six owners.

A problem occurs when he gets sick and is taken to the vet.

After that, the neighbors decide to feed Sid fewer meals.

The problem is solved when the neighbors get together and decide that Sid is the same cat that they have all been feeding.

The story ends when Sid moves to another street.

Name _____

Title:_____

Author:_____

This story takes place_____
_____
_____.
_____is an important character
in the story who_____
_____
_____.

A problem occurs when_____
_____
_____.

After that,_____
_____
_____.

The problem is solved when_____
_____
_____
_____.

The story ends when_____
_____
_____.

What's Cooking?

The What's Cooking? transparency offers an alternative to traditional story maps. Students can use this reproducible to organize and clarify their thoughts after reading a story or chapter book. Students first list the title and author of the book, then they write a short paragraph telling the setting under the *Equipment* heading. Under *Ingredients*, students name the characters in the story. The problem or plot is noted under *Mix*. Then, details about the solution to the problem are added under *Bake*. Finally, students write the story's ending under *Serve*. (See an example of a completed What's Cooking? transparency on the next page.)

Uses

- Many teachers hold a few individual conferences with students during the daily self-selected reading time while the rest of the class reads quietly. During these student conferences, use the What's Cooking? reproducible as an evaluation tool to check students' understanding of story elements. Discuss the different parts of the story and work with the students to help them fill in the information on the reproducible.

- As an after-reading activity, have students complete the reproducible either individually or in cooperative groups. Then, individuals or groups can share their responses with the class as you record the information on the transparency.

- Students can use the reproducible as a graphic organizer for their own writing. Have students fill in information for each of the different story elements, then use the completed form as a basis for creating their own stories.

Lessons

Using the book *Piggie Pie**, divide students into small-group discussion groups and give each group one copy of the What's Cooking? reproducible to review and fill out together. After a specific time limit, have all students come together and volunteer responses to each part of the reproducible. Write their answers on the transparency. You may want to write more than one response for each part and then have students as a group decide which response is best.

After reading *The Wolf's Chicken Stew***, have students fill in the What's Cooking reproducible. Then, invite students to fill in the reproducible again, this time creating their own recipe.

*Piggie Pie by Margie Palatini: Houghton Mifflin Co., 1997. (Picture book, ages 4-8, 32 pp.) A hungry witch descends on a barnyard with dreams of pork pie, only to find some strange chickens who are uncooperative about the whereabouts of the disappearing pigs.

***The Wolf's Chicken Stew* by Keiko Kasza: Paper Star, 1996. (Picture book, ages 4-8, 32 pp.) A hungry wolf's attempts to fatten a chicken for his stew pot have unexpected results.

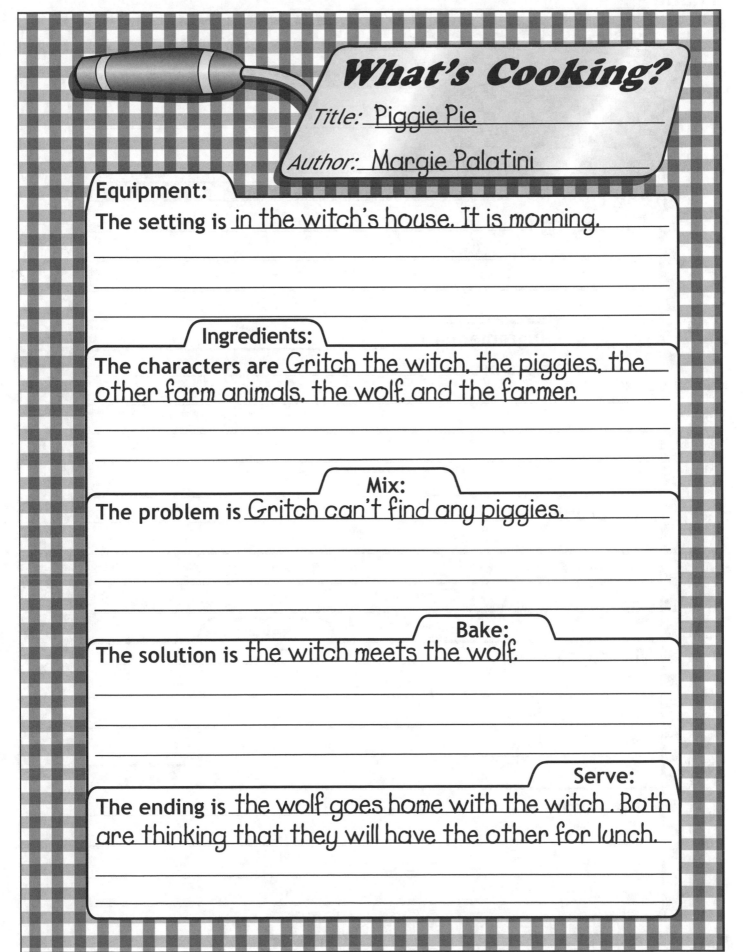

What's Cooking?

Title: Piggie Pie

Author: Margie Palatini

Equipment:

The setting is _in the witch's house. It is morning._

Ingredients:

The characters are _Gritch the witch, the piggies, the other farm animals, the wolf, and the farmer._

Mix:

The problem is _Gritch can't find any piggies._

Bake:

The solution is _the witch meets the wolf._

Serve:

The ending is _the wolf goes home with the witch. Both are thinking that they will have the other for lunch._

Name _____

What's Cooking?

Title: _____

Author: _____

Equipment:

The setting is _____

_____

_____

_____

Ingredients:

The characters are _____

_____

_____

_____

Mix:

The problem is _____

_____

_____

_____

Bake:

The solution is _____

_____

_____

_____

Serve:

The ending is _____

_____

_____

_____

Story Pyramid

The Story Pyramid provides a unique way to help students clarify their understanding of a book. Students first write the book title and author on the reproducible. The elements of the story form a pyramid shape when filled in according to the instructions. Students must think about the characters, setting, problems in the story, main events, and the solution to the story. (See an example of a completed Story Pyramid transparency on the next page.)

Uses

- During Guided Reading, students can do this exercise individually or in groups of four or less. For example, after partner reading or some other reading format, group the students, distribute a reproducible to each group, and give them a specified amount of time to complete the form. With the whole class together, call on groups to volunteer what they chose for each part of the pyramid and write their responses on the transparency.

- Have students use the pyramid as a graphic organizer to name the characters, settings, problems, and solutions for the featured books. This forces students to read for details concerning characters and story parts. After filling in the pyramid, students can use the reproducible as a guide for summarizing their books. The pyramid is in a story order, so students can proceed from the top to the bottom.

- Students can also use the form for a mystery book activity. Instruct each student to choose a book previously read and to fill in all the lines on the pyramid, leaving the *Title* and *Author* lines blank. Have students take turns identifying each student's book from the clues given.

Lesson

The Story Pyramid transparency could be used to profile an important person in history. (This could be especially useful for older or advanced students.) For example, the story pyramid could be completed as a profile on Martin Luther King, Jr.* after reading a biography or informational book about him.

The Story Pyramid transparency could also be used to summarize an important historical event after reading about it in your history or social studies text. For example, you may use the Story Pyramid to summarize the events that were part of settling the American West.

Line 1	pioneers	Line 5	they traveled in covered wagons
Line 2	brave strong	Line 6	many died from disease and accidents
Line 3	rough dangerous hard	Line 7	some set up towns in the West
Line 4	they wanted cheap farmland	Line 8	more and more people came to the West

Happy Birthday, Martin Luther King by Jean Marzollo: Scholastic, Inc., 1993. (Picture book, ages 4-8, 32 pp.) An easy-to-understand biography about Martin Luther King, Jr.

A Picture Book of Martin Luther King by David Adler: Holiday House, 1989. (Picture book, ages 4-8, 32 pp.) An introduction to the life of Martin Luther King, Jr.

Story Pyramid

Line 1: Name of the main character
Line 2: Two words describing the main character
Line 3: Three words describing the setting
Line 4: Four words stating the problem
Line 5: Five words describing the important event
Line 6: Six words describing a second important event
Line 7: Seven words describing a third important event
Line 8: Eight words stating the solution to the problem

Title: A Picture Book of
Martin Luther King
Author: David Adler

1   MLK, Jr.

2   minister peaceful

3 marches boycotts protests

4 African-Americans treated unfairly

5   MLK   made   a   famous   speech

6   led   civil   rights   march   on   Washington

7   he   was   shot   and   killed   in   Memphis

8 people began to treat African-Americans more fairly

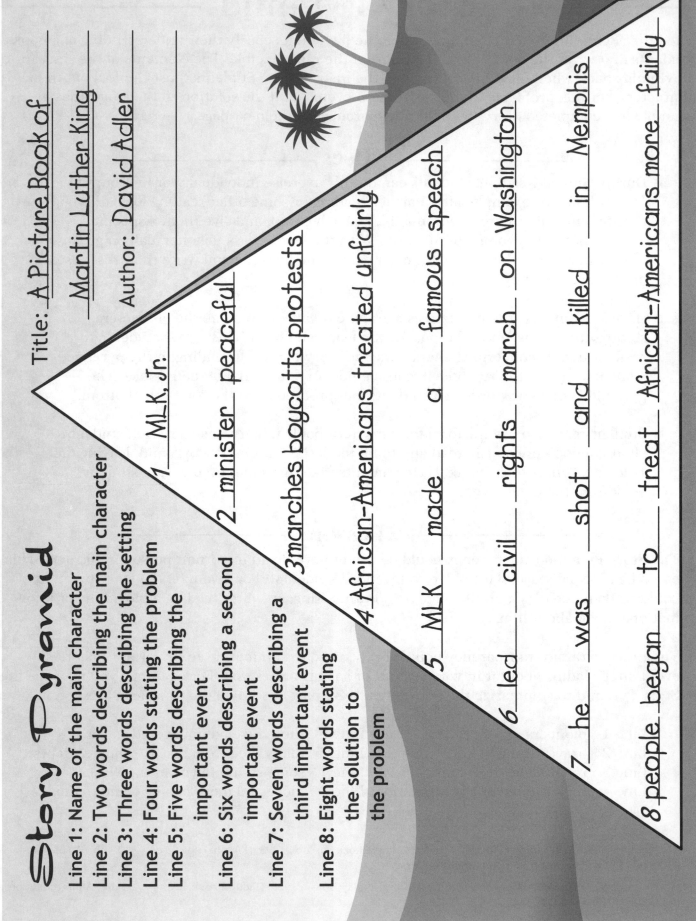

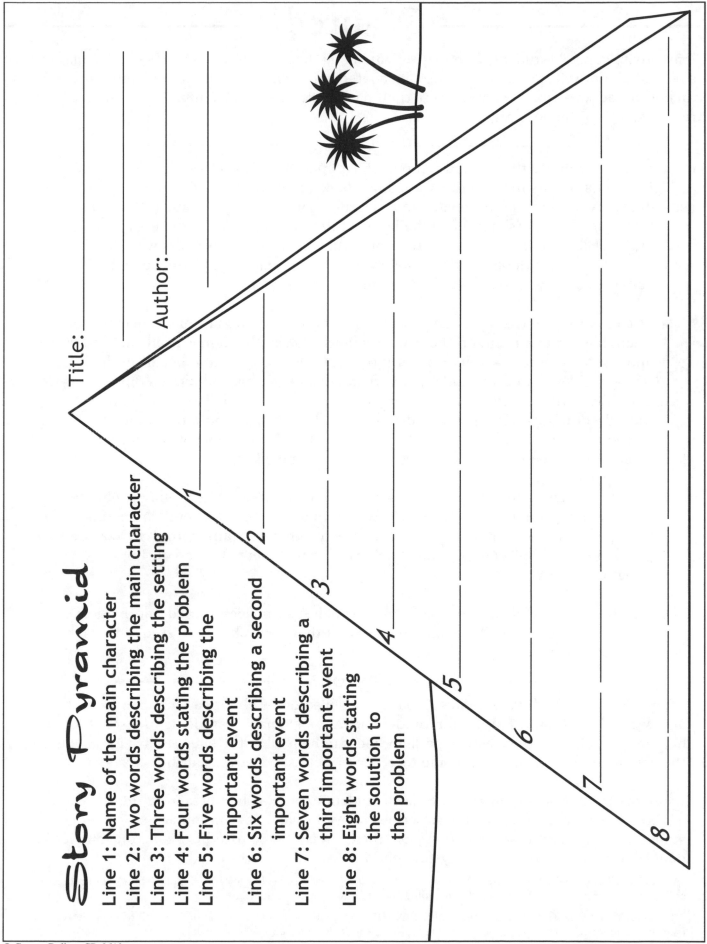

Story Pyramid

Line 1: Name of the main character

Line 2: Two words describing the main character

Line 3: Three words describing the setting

Line 4: Four words stating the problem

Line 5: Five words describing the important event

Line 6: Six words describing a second important event

Line 7: Seven words describing a third important event

Line 8: Eight words stating the solution to the problem

Title: _____

Author: _____

Wanted

This activity can help students formulate an understanding of characters in a book. You may choose to have students write about one of the main characters or a minor character. Examining characters can help students to create characters in their own stories. (See an example of a completed Wanted transparency on the next page.)

Uses

- Students can use the Wanted reproducible to play a *What Character Am I?* game. Instruct students to leave the *Name* line blank and to fill in the rest of the reproducible with information related to a favorite character from a book. (Have students write the characters' names on the backs of the sheets.) Hold up each paper in front of the class, reading the information for them, and let students guess who the character is. This is a good activity to follow up "getting acquainted with a character" activities done in Guided Reading lessons.

- Students can use the reproducibles to write about characters from a selected book. Then, have students cut off the name sections. Collect the names from each student and display them on a wall or bulletin board. Collect the remaining part of the reproducibles from each student. Mix them up and give each student a different one. Allow students to discuss which names on the wall or bulletin board match their descriptions, interests, and drawings on the sheets. Choose one student to display the reproducible next to the cut-out name. Then, the whole class discusses whether all the information matches the character chosen.

- Make a character book from the class's completed reproducibles. You may choose to create a book containing many characters from one book, or several characters from different books. Bind the reproducibles together with an appropriate cover and place in the reading center or in a book basket for students to read during self-selected reading time.

- Use the reproducible as a report form on which students can record information about a character, like Abraham Lincoln, that they have chosen to study in social studies or science.

Lessons

After reading *Arthur's Pet Business**, have pairs of students choose a character from the story and write about it on the Wanted reproducible. Ask each pair of students to discuss which character to choose. Have each pair share ideas to help fill in the sheets. Give a time limit for the activity, and have students come together as a class to share what they wrote.

Using the book, *Chocolatina***, have each student choose a character from the story to create a *What Character Am I?* sheet as described above in the first item under *Uses*. After giving students a specific time limit to complete the exercise, come together as a group and let students guess the identity of the mystery characters.

*Arthur's Pet Business by Marc Brown: Little Brown & Co., 1990. (Picture book, ages 4-8, 32 pp.) Arthur's pet business grows and grows until he has a lively menagerie, including an ant farm and a boa constrictor.

**Chocolatina by Erik Kraft: Bridgewater Books, 1998. (Picture book, preschool, 32 pp.) Tina's health teacher always admonishes her students, "You are what you eat!" One morning Tina wakes up a completely chocolate girl!

WANTED

Name: Abraham Lincoln

Age: 52 (when he became president)

Draw a picture of the character here.

Description: He was very tall. He grew a beard after a little girl wrote to him and suggested he would win the election if he did.

Interests: He liked to read. As a young man, he walked long distances to borrow books. He had a dog named Jib, a cat named Bob, and a turkey named Jack.

WANTED

Name:_____

Age:_____

Draw a picture of the character here.

Description:_____

_____

_____

Interests:_____

_____

_____

_____

Everyone Read To...

Everyone Read To... (ERT)* is an activity in which the teacher sets a purpose for reading and decides how much students read. When the information for which the students are reading is stated directly on the page, they are reading to *find out*. When students have to make inferences about what they have read in order to meet the purpose, they are reading to *figure out*. For example, you may choose to instruct the class, *Everyone read to find out the name of the main character's best friend.* Write the purpose in the first box on the transparency. Tell students to scan the text and pictures in the book and raise their hands when they know the answer. Write the students' responses on the transparency. (See an example of a completed Everyone Read To... transparency on the next page.)

Uses

- Write specific purposes on the ERT reproducible, duplicate it for students, and ask them to find the answers in the book. Students could also be divided into groups for this activity. Once the questions are answered, have students share some of their responses.

- Students can use the ERT reproducible during Literature Circles. Literature Circles are small, cooperative groups of students who choose books to read and discuss the books within their groups. Since children in Literature Circles should read on their own, rather than reading aloud with the group members, make sure students can read their books without help. Children in Literature Circles have different roles and can choose the role they want. These roles determine their purpose for reading. There are a variety of roles, such as *Connector, Illustrator, Discussion Director, Passage Master, and Vocabulary Enricher.* Have each student write his thoughts related to his specific role on the reproducible. For example, the Passage Master might write a purpose such as, *Read to find out what is the most unusual event in the story.*

Lessons

After you have used the ERT reproducibles in Literature Circles (see above use), collect the papers from the students who chose to be *Vocabulary Enrichers*. Vocabulary Enrichers should find words that are new, important, or puzzling. List these words for the class and ask students to find the sentences from the book where the words are used.

As students read *The Wolf's Chicken Stew*** for the first time, project the ERT transparency with purposes added such as: *Read to find out... why the Wolf was baking,* or *...what happened when he went to check on the hen?* Uncover only one question at a time. As students find answers, write the answers on the transparency, and then uncover the next question. Ask questions in sequential story order.

*Everyone Read To... (ERT) is a strategy developed by Dr. Patricia Cunningham. For more information, please refer to *Guided Reading the Four-Blocks™ Way* (CD-2407).

**The Wolf's Chicken Stew* by Keiko Kasza: Paper Star, 1996. (Picture book, ages 4-8, 32 pp.) A hungry wolf's attempts to fatten a chicken for his stew pot have unexpected results.

Everyone Read To...

Read to find out... why the wolf was baking.

We found out... the wolf wanted to fatten the hen and eat her.

Read to find out... what happened when he went to check on the hen.

We found out... the wolf was surprised to find the hen and chicks to be so friendly.

Read to figure out... the main idea of this story.

We figured out... that even though in the beginning, the wolf tries to do something bad, he makes new friends in the end.

Name _____

Everyone Read To...

Read to find out...

We found out...

Read to find out...

We found out...

Read to figure out...

We figured out...

Who? What Did They Do?

This transparency provides practice in identifying main characters and summarizing stories. Have students fill out the reproducible either individually or in cooperative groups. Instruct them to write the character's name in the first box and to write a short summary of the book in the large box. After a specific amount of time, ask for the name of the main character of the story, and write it on the transparency. Then, ask for volunteers to read their summaries. Write as many summaries as possible on the transparency. Allow the class to decide which is the best summary for the book. (See an example of a completed Who? What Did They Do? transparency on the next page.)

Uses

■ Use the reproducible as a way to check students' comprehension of a book. Younger students might write the character's name, a sentence, and draw a picture to summarize the story.

■ During Guided Reading time, have students use the reproducible to develop an overall picture of a book. Have each student name a character or a group of characters. Instruct students to make story outlines using the words *beginning*, *middle*, and *end* and to write sentences under each. Allow students to use the reproducible as a guide for discussing their books in Literature Circles.

■ When introducing students to report writing about famous historical figures, let them use the Who? What Did They Do? reproducible as a graphic organizer. Then, students can use the information from the reproducible to complete their reports.

Lessons

Using the book *The True Story of the Three Little Pigs!*, ask students to name the main character—Alexander T. Wolf. Then, have students create a summary of the story. Ask students to think of a good beginning, middle, and end; or a good beginning, the problem, and how it is solved. Ask for volunteers to share what they have written, and write student responses on the transparency. Students can then decide as a group the best elements to include in the story summary.

After reading a biography or other historical book during Guided Reading, use the Who? What Did They Do? transparency to profile an important person in history. For example, after reading *Explorers (Women in Profile Series)*** or other nonfiction sources***, ask students to help fill in the transparency with information about Valentina Tereshkova, a Russian cosmonaut who became the first woman to travel in space when she piloted the 1963 Vostok 6 mission.

The True Story of the Three Little Pigs! by Jon Scieszka: Penguin Putnam Books for Young Readers, 1996. (Picture book, ages 5-12, 32 pp.) The wolf gives his own outlandish version of what really happened when he tangled with the three little pigs.

**Explorers (Women in Profile Series)* by Carlotta Hacker: Crabtree Publisher, 1988. (Informational book, ages 9-12, 48 pp.) Provides in-depth and numerous brief profiles of six 20th-century women who have made significant contributions to their fields. Other titles in the series include: *Musicians, Nobel Prize Winners, Political Leaders, Scientists, Writers.*

***America's Daughters: 400 Years of American Women* by Judith Head: Perspective Publications, 1999. (Informational book, ages 9-12, 128 pp.) Overview of women in American history from 1600 to present. Includes many names left out of other sources.

***Girls Think of Everything: Stories of Ingenious Inventions by Women* by Catherine Thimmesh: Houghton Mifflin Co., 2000. (Informational book, ages 9-12, 64 pp.) Inventions of ten women and two girls are explored, from the most practical (windshield wipers) to the best-loved (chocolate chip cookies).

Who?
What Did They Do?

Character

Alexander T. Wolf

(from The True Story of the Three Little Pigs!

by Jon Scieszka)

Summary

Alexander T. Wolf wants to bake a cake for his granny, but he doesn't have any sugar. He tries to borrow a cup of sugar from his neighbors, the three little pigs. The wolf has a bad cold and when he sneezes, he blows down the first little pig's straw house. Then, he eats the little pig. He goes to the second little pig's stick house, and the same thing happens! The wolf goes to the third little pig's brick house. The third little pig makes the wolf mad, so the wolf tries to break down the door. The police come and put the wolf in jail.

Name _____

Who?
What Did They Do?

Character

Summary

Story Structure

The Story Structure transparency can help students to realize that a story always has a beginning, middle, and end. Use this transparency as an after-reading activity to organize the events in a book the class has read. Ask students to tell in their own words the beginning, middle, and end of the story. The reproducible can also help students clarify their own thoughts about a story they are writing. (See an example of a completed Story Structure transparency on the next page.)

Uses

■ Students can use the reproducible as a way of expressing (in their own words) the beginning, middle, and end of the book they are reading during Guided Reading. Each student writes each part, and then shares his ideas with the class. Allow students to decide as a class which beginning, middle, and end best represent the story. Write the chosen elements on the transparency.

■ Pair students with partners, then have each set of partners choose a book and work together to write its beginning, middle, and end on the reproducible. Have students cut the sections apart. Collect only the beginnings from each pair of partners and post them on a wall or bulletin board. Then, collect the other sections. Distribute two sections (a mixed *middle* and *end*) to each set of partners. Each pair decides which *beginning* section posted on the wall relates to the *middle* section they are holding. When all pairs have posted the correct *middle* sections, allow the pairs to post the *end* sections. This is a good after-reading activity, and could also be used to compare two similar books. Alternatively, at the end of a unit where several books have been read, each student could select one book and then write its beginning, middle, and end.

■ Give each student a reproducible. Have students write a good beginning, middle, and end to the book they have been reading during Guided Reading, then cut the sections apart and paste them on 9" x 18" construction paper, positioned horizontally. Instruct students to draw pictures above each section representing that part of the story.

■ For conferencing time or small discussion groups, students can use the reproducible to organize their ideas for a book they will be discussing or sharing.

Lesson

Using the book, *Mitchell is Moving**, have students write a good beginning, middle, and end to the story. Cut the sections apart and paste them at the bottom of a 9" x 18" sheet of paper, positioned horizontally. Above each section, have students illustrate what they wrote.

Mitchell is Moving by M.W. Sharmat: Econo-Clad Books, 1999. (Picture book, ages 4-8, 47 pp.) Mitchell the dinosaur is tired of living in the same, old place and decides to move "three days away." His best friend Margo thinks of ingenious ways to keep Mitchell as her neighbor.

Story Structure

Title: Mitchell Is Moving

Author: M.W. Sharmat

Beginning Mitchell is a dinosaur who is tired of living in the same old place and decides to move away.

Middle Margo, his neighbor and best friend, is unhappy about it and doesn't want him to move. She tries to think of ways to get him to stay. Mitchell moves anyway.

End Margo goes to visit Mitchell. She still misses him and finally moves next door to Mitchell.

Name _____

Story Structure

Title: _____

Author: _____

Beginning _____
_____
_____
_____
_____

Middle _____
_____
_____
_____
_____

End _____
_____
_____
_____

Story Sequence

The Story Sequence transparency helps students to understand the most important events in a text and that those events occur in a certain sequence. Using "time-order" words such as *first*, *next*, *then*, and *last*, help students to organize their thoughts. (See an example of a completed Story Sequence transparency on the next page.)

Uses

- Use this transparency after reading a book to see how much students know about what happened in the text, and when it happened.

- Use the Story Sequence transparency to support the Everyone Read To... strategy. Write what students are to first read for in the section marked *First*, while they read the page and record their answers on the reproducible. For example, you might write *Read page three to find out what the main character needed at the store.* When all sections are filled in, use the completed page to discuss the story.

- After completing the Story Sequence transparency for a book, ask students to help identify and explain any cause and effect relationships between the events listed.

- Have students make predictions about the text based on a picture walk of the text. Write students' predictions on the transparency. Then, read the book as a class and decide whether or not the predictions were correct.

Lessons

After studying a book, use the Story Sequence reproducible to evaluate students' comprehension of the story. Have students write in their own words the story parts as they happened. Alternately, write four parts to the story (out of order) on the Story Sequence transparency. Then, have students copy the parts to the correct places on their Story Sequence reproducible.

Use the Story Sequence reproducible to list the sequence of a major historical event. Another alternative is to list the important steps of a simple science experiment. The following experiment will illustrate how frost collects on cold surfaces.

First... place ½ cup rock salt and 2 cups crushed ice in a 1 lb. coffee can.
Next... stir vigorously.
Then... allow the can to sit for 30 to 40 minutes.
Last... observe the surface of the can.

Story Sequence

Title: Arthur's TV Trouble

Author: Marc Brown

First... Arthur was watching TV and saw an ad for Treat-Timers.

Next... Arthur wanted a job to make money to buy a Treat-Timer.

Then... Arthur stacked newspapers for money, but the wind began to blow them away.

Last... Arthur and D.W. restack the newspapers, are paid for the job, and buy the Treat-Timer at the mall. The Treat-Timer doesn't work, so Arthur finds another product on a TV commercial to buy.

Story Sequence

Title: _____

Author: _____

First...

Next...

Then...

Last...

Time-Order Words

This transparency is for introducing and practicing time-order words such as *first, then, next, after that, finally,* and *last.* The exercise helps students to see how important these words are to clarify the sequence of a story. Discuss how a reader might not understand when events happened in a story without time-order words. Learning to follow a story's sequence is a comprehension strategy which helps students know what to expect in the story, and increases their understanding and enjoyment. (See an example of a completed Time-Order Words transparency on the next page.)

Uses

- Students can use the reproducible as a guide to find the same words in books featured in Guided Reading. Have students write the sentences from the story (in order) on the reproducible to see the sequence of events.

- Have younger students cut the time-order words apart, mix them up, then rearrange the story and paste it to a piece of construction paper in the correct order.

- If the majority of your students have not used time-order words in their summarizing, use this transparency to introduce this helpful strategy. Students can then use the reproducible to help with their own writing.

- Even after using this reproducible the first time with students, there may be times during the year when students need to review how these particular words can help them organize their thoughts for discussion groups, summarizing, and book review.

Lessons

Read *Peanut Butter and Jelly: A Play Rhyme** aloud to the class and then have students use the reproducible to write their own recipes for a peanut butter and jelly sandwich. If desired, students can make the sandwiches as a treat.

After reading *The Furry News: How to Make a Newspaper***, children can use the reproducible to list the instructions for making a newspaper (in their own words). If desired, allow students to make a class newspaper. Assign roles to students such as editor, writer, illustrator, etc.

**Peanut Butter and Jelly: A Play Rhyme* by Nadine Bernard Westcott: Econo-Clad Books, 1999. (Picture book, ages 4-8, 32 pp.) A favorite play rhyme takes on gigantic proportions as two children create a table-sized sandwich from scratch.

***The Furry News: How to Make a Newspaper* by Loreen Leedy: Holiday House, 1990. (Picture book, ages 4-8, 32 pp.) Big Bear and his animal friends make their own newspaper and teach young readers how to create their own.

Time-Order Words

Title: The Furry News   Author: Loreen Leedy

First, the animals decided to make their own newspaper.

Then, Big Bear gave every animal a job.

Next, each reporter gathered all the facts.

After that, they sold space in the newspaper for advertisements.

Finally, the printer made many copies.

Last, they were delivered right away.

Name _____

Time-Order Words

Title: _____ Author: _____

First, _____
_____
_____.

Then, _____
_____
_____

Next, _____
_____
_____.

After that, _____
_____
_____.

Finally, _____
_____
_____.

Last, _____
_____
_____.

Filmstrip Story Sequencer

As an alternative to using a story map, students can use the Filmstrip Story Sequencer to review a Guided Reading book. *Strip 1* can be used to write the title and author of the book. *Strip 2* can be the beginning of the story. *Strip 3* can be used to write the problem. Tell how the problem was solved in *Strip 4*. *Strip 5* can be used to write the ending or a summary of the book. (See an example of a completed Filmstrip Story Sequencer transparency on the next page.)

Uses

- Have students read a book in pairs, and then work with their partners to write the parts of the story on the reproducible. Call the whole group back together, and let students volunteer information for you to write on the transparency. You may want to include more than one idea for each part, and then after all the parts have been discussed, have students determine the best representation for that part of the story.

- The Filmstrip Story Sequencer can also be used during after-reading activities when students are formulating ideas about books they have read. You may decide, for instance, that *Strip 1* will be the title, *Strip 2* the setting, *Strip 3* the problem, *Strip 4* the solution, and *Strip 5* the ending. Students can use the reproducible as a graphic organizer and review the book with this guide in mind.

- Younger students can represent story parts by writing short sentences and drawing pictures in each section.

- Students can write the story sequence in each section, cut the sections apart, draw pictures to represent each part of the story, then place each section under the pictures representing that part of the story.

- Write the story sequence out-of-order, cut out the rectangular sections containing the story elements (covering the numbers), and then have students put the sections in the correct sequence.

Lessons

Select four different books with a common author, topic, theme, etc. Read aloud the first several pages of each book, then allow students to rank their favorites. Divide the class into book club groups based on the students' choices. Let the book club groups meet to read and discuss the books, while you rotate through the groups offering support as needed. Have each group fill out the reproducible about their book, then perform a skit for the class based on that information.

Have students create their own "movies." As a class, determine the correct sequence for a book that has been read. Write the correct sequence on the transparency. Then, give each student a copy of the reproducible. Ask students to draw pictures to represent the sequence of events in the book—one scene or picture in each section. Bind the completed "movie pages" together to create a class book for students to enjoy in a reading center or during self-selected reading time.

Filmstrip Story Sequencer

1

The Teacher from the Black Lagoon
by Mike Thaler

2

The boy is going to school on the first day and he is wondering who his teacher might be.

3

He begins daydreaming that the teacher might be many horrible things.

4

The boy dreams that many different things happen to his classmates.

5

In the end, he awakes to find that his new teacher is a very loving person.

Name _____

Filmstrip Story Sequencer

1

2

3

4

5